COLOR BIBLE

Verses about

Faith

A BIBLE VERSE COLORING BOOK

Date : _____

TO : _____

From : _____

I WRITE THESE THINGS TO YOU

who believe in the name of the son of God

So that you may know that
you have eternal life.

1 John 5:13

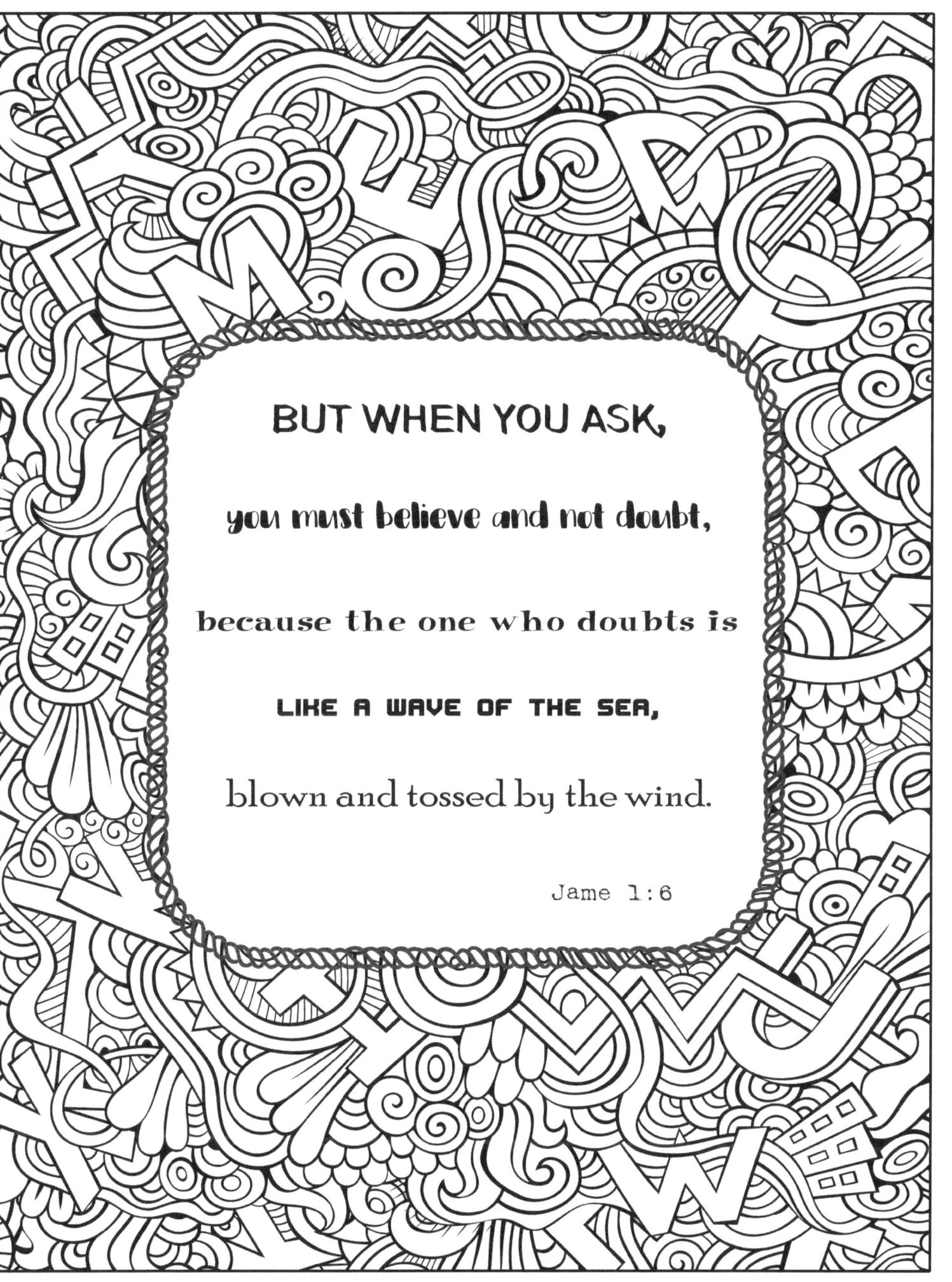

BUT WHEN YOU ASK,

you must believe and not doubt,

because the one who doubts is

LIKE A WAVE OF THE SEA,

blown and tossed by the wind.

Jame 1:6

For God so loved the world that he gave this one and only son, that whoever believes in him shall not PERISH BUT HAVE ETERNAL LIFE.

John 3:16

Whoever believes in the Son has eternal life,

but whoever rejects the Son

will not see life,

FOR GOD'S WRATH REMAINS ON THEM.

John 3:36

Then Jesus declared, "I am the bread of life.

Whoever comes to me will never go hungry

AND WHOEVER

believes in me will never be thirsty.

John 6:35

Whoever believes in me,

as Scripture has said...

RIVERS OF LIVING WATER

will flow from within them."

John 7:38

I have chosen the way of faithfulness; I have set my heart on your laws.

Psalm 119:30

Then Jesus said,

"Did I not tell you that

If you believe,

you will see the glory of God?"

John 11:40

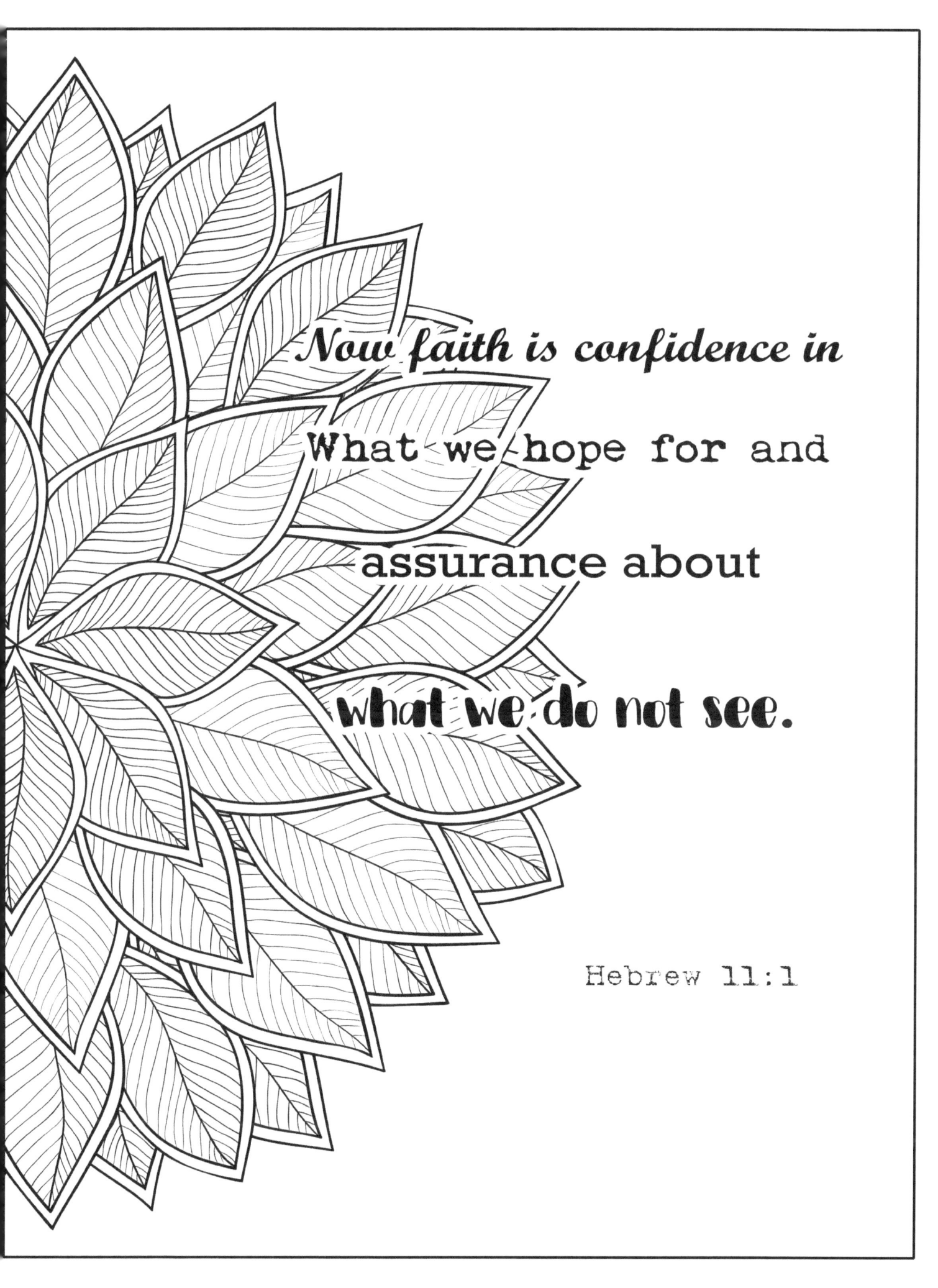

Now faith is confidence in What we hope for and assurance about what we do not see.

Hebrew 11:1

in the hope of eternal life,

which God,

Who does not lie,

promised before

the beginning of time,

Titus 1:2

For we live by faith, not by sight.

2 Corinthians 5:7

BE ON YOUR GUARD,

stand firm in the faith;

be courangeous; be strong

1 Corinthians 16:13

FOR EVERYONE BORN OF GOD

OVERCOME THE WORLD.

This is the victory that

HAS OVERCOME THE WORLD, EVEN OUR FAITH.

1 John 5:4

THEREFORE, BROTHERS AND SISTERS,

in all our distress and persecution

we were encouraged about you

BECAUE OF YOUR FAITH.

1 Thessalonians 3:7

Not that we lord it over your faith,

BUT WE WORK WITH YOU FOR YOUR JOY

because it is by faith you stand firm.

2 Corinthians 1:24

I have fought the good fight.

I HAVE FINISHED THE RACE,

I have kept the faith.

2 Timothy 4:7

For it is by grace you have been saved,

through faith—and this is not from yourselves,

it is the gift of God —

Ephesians 2:8

In Addition to all this, take up the shield of faith,

with which you can extinguish all the flaming

arrows of the evil one.

Ephesians 6:16

For through the Spirit we eagerly await by,

faith the righteousness for which we hope.

Galatians 5:5

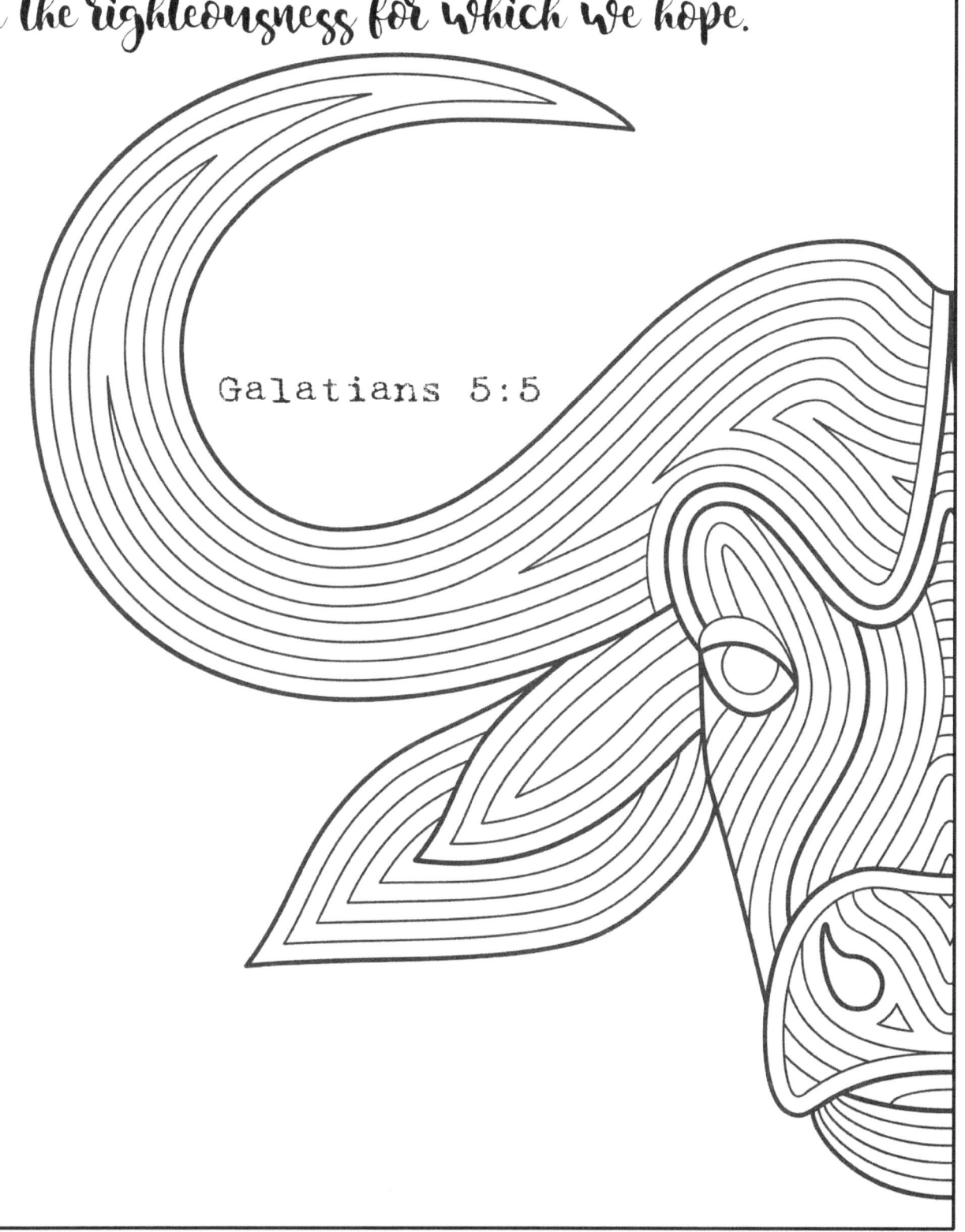

Because you know that

the testing of your faith produces perseverance.

James 1:3

For with God nothing shall be impossible.

Luke 1:37

For We walk by Faith, not by Sight;

2 Corinthians 5:7

Join Us >> bit.ly/get_sample_free

- Get Free "Reviw Copies" of our New releases
- Exclusive offers and book giveaways
- More events from our community

Thank you